Cooking Light.

SALADS & DRESSINGS

Cooking Light®

SALADS & DRESSINGS

80 Delightfully Different Recipes

WARNER BOOKS

A Time Warner Company

PHOTOGRAPHER: *Jim Bathie*

PHOTO STYLIST: *Kay E. Clarke*

BOOK DESIGN: *Giorgetta Bell McRee*

COVER DESIGN: *Andrew Newman*

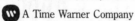

Warner Books, Inc., 666 Fifth Avenue, New York, NY 10103

W A Time Warner Company

Printed in the United States of America
First printing: February 1991
10 9 8 7 6 5 4 3 2 1

Library of Congress Cataloging-in-Publication Data

Cooking light salads and dressings.
   p.   cm.—(Cooking light)
Includes index.
ISBN 0–446–39185–9
1. Salads. 2. Salad dressing. I. Title: Salads and dressings.
II. Series: Cooking light (New York, N.Y.)
TX740.C655 1991
641.8'3—dc20   90–12861
                                                     CIP

CONTENTS

EATING WELL IS THE BEST REWARD

Welcome to **Cooking Light**, a cookbook that celebrates the pleasures of good health. These low-fat, low-calorie recipes are easy to make, a delight to behold, and a feast for the senses.

Guided by the belief that good health and good food are synonymous, **Cooking Light** provides an approach to eating and cooking that is both healthy and appealing. Using the eighty recipes in this book, you will see how easy it is to minimize fat and sodium while maximizing minerals, fiber, and vitamins. And you will be delighted by the emphasis on the good taste and texture of fresh wholesome food cooked the light way.

So eat hearty, slim down and delight yourself, your family, and your friends with these easy-to-prepare, all-natural, and very delicious recipes.

EDITOR'S NOTE

Unless otherwise indicated:

eggs are large

margarine is corn oil margarine

sugar is granulated white sugar

flour is all-purpose

raisins are "dark"

cranberries and other ingredients are fresh

prepared mustard is regular store-bought yellow mustard

all noodles are cooked without fat or salt

Dutch process cocoa is alkalized

chicken breast is cooked without skin and without salt

vinegar is regular distilled vinegar

Cooking Light.

SALADS & DRESSINGS

VEGETABLE, BEAN AND GRAIN SALADS

BAKED SONOMA GOAT CHEESE SALAD

½ cup soft breadcrumbs
½ teaspoon dried whole thyme
1 (5½-ounce) log fresh goat cheese, cut into 6 equal
  rounds
2 cups torn romaine lettuce
2 cups torn Bibb lettuce
2 cups torn radicchio
Vinaigrette (recipe follows)

Combine breadcrumbs and thyme; toss gently. Coat cheese
rounds with breadcrumb mixture; place on ungreased baking
sheet. Bake at 400° for 10 minutes or until lightly browned.
Remove from oven, and set aside.

  Combine lettuces and vinaigrette; toss lightly. Arrange lettuce
mixture on 6 individual salad plates. Place 1 reserved round of
cheese on top of lettuce. Serve immediately. Yield: 6 servings (122
calories per serving).

Vinaigrette:

3 tablespoons red wine vinegar
2 tablespoons water
1 teaspoon Dijon mustard
1 clove garlic, crushed
1 tablespoon olive oil

Combine vinegar, water, mustard, and crushed garlic in a small bowl; stir with a wire whisk until well blended. Stir in olive oil. Yield: ¼ cup plus 2 tablespoons.

PROTEIN 5.2 / FAT 8.2 / CARBOHYDRATE 6.8 / CHOLESTEROL 23 / IRON 0.8 / SODIUM 361 / CALCIUM 144

CAESAR SALAD

2 slices thinly sliced white bread
Vegetable cooking spray
½ teaspoon garlic powder
1 clove garlic, halved
4 cups shredded romaine lettuce
2 eggs
¼ teaspoon dry mustard
3 tablespoons lemon juice
2 tablespoons water
2 teaspoons olive oil
2 teaspoons Worcestershire sauce
2 tablespoons grated Parmesan cheese
½ teaspoon cracked pepper

Coat bread lightly with cooking spray. Sprinkle with garlic powder. Place on an ungreased baking sheet. Bake at 300° for 20 minutes or until bread is golden brown. Cut bread into cubes, and set aside.

Rub inside of a large bowl with garlic halves; discard garlic. Place lettuce in bowl.

Pour water to a depth of 2 inches in a medium saucepan; bring water to a boil, and turn off heat. Carefully lower eggs into water using a slotted spoon; let stand 1 minute. Remove eggs from water and let cool.

Combine prepared eggs, dry mustard, lemon juice, 2 tablespoons water, olive oil, and Worcestershire sauce, stirring well. Drizzle egg mixture over lettuce in bowl. Sprinkle with Parmesan cheese and pepper; toss lightly. Top evenly with reserved bread cubes. Yield: 8 servings (62 calories per ½-cup serving).

PROTEIN 3.2 / FAT 3.3 / CARBOHYDRATE 5.1 / CHOLESTEROL 70 / IRON 0.8 / SODIUM 87 / CALCIUM 42

NOUVELLE TOSSED SALAD

1 clove garlic, split
7 cups torn curly endive
3 cups torn radicchio
2 cups arugula leaves
3 tablespoons vinegar
2 tablespoons walnut oil
¼ teaspoon salt-free herb and spice seasoning
⅛ teaspoon pepper
Tomato rose (optional)

Rub a large salad bowl with garlic. Discard garlic. Combine endive, radicchio, and arugula in salad bowl, and toss well. Cover and chill thoroughly.

Combine vinegar, oil, seasoning, and pepper in a jar; cover tightly, and shake vigorously. Pour over chilled salad, and toss well. Garnish with tomato rose, if desired. Yield: 12 servings (30 calories per serving).

PROTEIN 0.6 / FAT 2.4 / CARBOHYDRATE 1.9 / CHOLESTEROL 0 / IRON 0.4 / SODIUM 9 / CALCIUM 28

SWEET POTATO AMBROSIA SALAD

3 medium-size sweet potatoes (1½ pounds)
1 cup cubed fresh pineapple, well drained
1 medium orange, sectioned and well drained
2 tablespoons low-fat sour cream
2 tablespoons plain nonfat yogurt
2 tablespoons reduced-calorie mayonnaise
1 tablespoon plus 1½ teaspoons grated coconut
1 tablespoon honey
½ teaspoon grated orange rind
1 tablespoon unsweetened orange juice
¼ teaspoon coconut extract
⅛ teaspoon salt
Fresh mint sprig (optional)

Wrap sweet potatoes in aluminum foil; bake at 400° for 45 minutes or until tender. Cool completely. Remove and discard skin; cut potatoes into cubes. Combine sweet potatoes, pineapple, and orange sections in a serving bowl; toss gently, and set aside.

Combine sour cream and remaining ingredients, except mint, in a small bowl, stirring well. Pour over reserved sweet potato mixture; toss gently. Cover and chill 2 hours. Garnish with mint, if desired. Yield: 8 servings (120 calories per serving).

PROTEIN 1.8 / FAT 2.4 / CARBOHYDRATE 23.8 / CHOLESTEROL 3 / IRON 0.6 / SODIUM 78 / CALCIUM 34

MEXICAN DINNER SALAD

2 cups torn red leaf lettuce
2 cups torn romaine lettuce
1 cup cubed avocado
1 cup jicama, peeled and cut into ¼-inch strips
4 fresh tomatillos, husked and chopped
¼ cup tomato juice with green chiles
1 tablespoon red wine vinegar
2 teaspoons vegetable oil
¼ teaspoon sugar

Combine first 5 ingredients in a large bowl; set aside. Combine tomato juice, vinegar, vegetable oil, and sugar in a small bowl, mixing well. Pour dressing over salad, and toss well. Serve immediately. Yield: 6 servings (59 calories per serving).

PROTEIN 1.3 / FAT 4.2 / CARBOHYDRATE 4.8 / CHOLESTEROL 0 / IRON 0.6 / SODIUM 61 / CALCIUM 15

MOROCCAN CARROT SALAD

3 pounds carrots, scraped and diagonally sliced
2¼ cups water
½ cup lemon juice
3 tablespoons red wine vinegar
8 cloves garlic, crushed
1 teaspoon salt
½ teaspoon red pepper
Fresh dill sprigs (optional)

Combine carrots and water to cover in a large Dutch oven. Cover and bring to a boil. Boil 6 minutes or until crisp-tender. Drain carrots, and place in a large shallow dish.

Combine 2¼ cups water, lemon juice, red wine vinegar, garlic, salt, and red pepper; pour over carrots. Cover and refrigerate 8 hours or overnight. Drain off marinade. Place carrots in a large serving bowl, and garnish with fresh dill sprigs, if desired. Yield: 16 servings (41 calories per serving).

PROTEIN 1.0 / FAT 0.2 / CARBOHYDRATE 9.8 / CHOLESTEROL 0 / IRON 0.5 / SODIUM 177 / CALCIUM 27

SPECIAL ROMAINE SALAD

1 (14-ounce) can artichoke hearts, drained and quartered
1 (14-ounce) can hearts of palm, drained and sliced into
    ½-inch pieces
1 medium onion, thinly sliced and separated into rings
½ cup white wine vinegar
¼ cup water
1 tablespoon olive or vegetable oil
¼ teaspoon pepper
¼ teaspoon dried whole oregano
1 clove garlic, crushed
1 (10-ounce) head romaine lettuce, torn
8 cherry tomatoes, halved
2 tablespoons grated Parmesan cheese

Combine artichokes, hearts of palm, and onion in a shallow baking dish. Combine vinegar and next 5 ingredients in a glass jar; cover tightly, and shake vigorously. Pour over vegetable mixture, tossing well. Cover and refrigerate 8 hours or overnight, tossing occasionally.

Drain vegetable mixture, reserving marinade. Combine lettuce and marinated vegetables in a large salad bowl; toss gently. Arrange cherry tomatoes on top of salad, and sprinkle with Parmesan cheese. Serve with reserved marinade, if desired. Yield: 12 servings (53 calories per 1-cup serving).

PROTEIN 1.9 / FAT 1.8 / CARBOHYDRATE 9.5 / FIBER 1.4 / CHOLESTEROL 0 / SODIUM 75 / POTASSIUM 237

HERB-GARLIC POTATO SALAD

1½ pounds red potatoes, cut into ¾-inch cubes
3 cups water
3 tablespoons plain low-fat yogurt
2 tablespoons sour cream
2 teaspoons Dijon mustard
1 clove garlic, minced
1 teaspoon dried whole basil
¼ teaspoon salt
¼ teaspoon dried whole thyme

Combine potatoes and the water in a large saucepan; bring to a boil. Cover; reduce heat, and simmer 8 minutes or just until tender. Drain and transfer to a large bowl.

Combine yogurt, sour cream, mustard, garlic, basil, salt, and thyme in a small bowl; stir until well blended. Pour over potatoes, and toss gently until well coated. Serve warm or chilled. Yield: 8 servings (86 calories per serving).

PROTEIN 2.0 / FAT 1.0 / CARBOHYDRATE 17.8 / FIBER 0.4 / CHOLESTEROL 2 / SODIUM 95 / POTASSIUM 303

GUACAMOLE SALAD

1 (10-ounce) avocado, peeled and chopped
½ cup evaporated skim milk
3 tablespoons lemon juice
2 tablespoons sour cream
1 clove garlic, crushed
¼ teaspoon salt
¼ teaspoon chili powder
¼ teaspoon Worcestershire sauce
⅛ teaspoon ground cumin
2 drops hot sauce
1 (1-pound) head iceberg lettuce, shredded
¼ pound fresh spinach, shredded
1 (15-ounce) can garbanzo beans, drained
1 (14-ounce) can hearts of palm, drained and sliced
1 small sweet red or green pepper, seeded and chopped

Combine first 10 ingredients in container of an electric blender; process until smooth.

Combine lettuce, spinach, garbanzo beans, and hearts of palm in a large salad bowl; toss lightly. Spoon onto individual salad plates. Top evenly with avocado mixture, and garnish with red pepper. Yield: 8 servings (150 calories per serving).

PROTEIN 5.5 / FAT 7.4 / CARBOHYDRATE 19.6 / FIBER 5.2 / CHOLESTEROL 2 / SODIUM 307 / POTASSIUM 675

MARINATED GREEN BEAN SALAD

1 pound fresh green beans
1 (2-ounce) jar sliced pimiento, drained
1 medium tomato, chopped
½ cup chopped green pepper
½ cup reduced-calorie Italian salad dressing
¼ cup chopped fresh parsley
¼ teaspoon freshly ground pepper

Remove strings from green beans; wash thoroughly. Cut each bean lengthwise into 4 strips. Place in a steaming rack over boiling water. Cover and steam 5 minutes or until crisp-tender. Cool completely.

Combine beans, pimiento, tomato, and green pepper in a shallow container. Combine salad dressing, parsley, and pepper; stir well. Pour over bean mixture. Cover and refrigerate overnight. Yield: 6 servings (43 calories per serving).

PROTEIN 1.9 / FAT 0.3 / CARBOHYDRATE 9.7 / FIBER 2.0 / CHOLESTEROL 0 / SODIUM 190 / POTASSIUM 26

FRUITY CABBAGE SALAD

4 cups shredded cabbage
1 (8-ounce) can unsweetened pineapple tidbits, drained
1 medium pear, cored and diced
1 medium-size Red Delicious apple, cored and diced
½ cup seedless green grapes, halved
1 (8-ounce) carton plain low-fat yogurt
2 teaspoons cider vinegar
1 teaspoon honey
½ teaspoon celery seeds
1 medium banana, sliced

Combine first 5 ingredients. Combine yogurt, vinegar, honey, and celery seeds, stirring well; pour over cabbage mixture, tossing to coat well. Cover and chill 1 hour. Add banana just before serving, and toss to coat. Yield: 12 servings (54 calories per ½-cup serving).

PROTEIN 1.6 / FAT 0.6 / CARBOHYDRATE 11.9 / FIBER 1.3 / CHOLESTEROL 1 / SODIUM 18 / POTASSIUM 199

ENDIVE SALAD WITH PIMIENTO DRESSING

¼ cup red wine vinegar
1 (2-ounce) jar sliced pimiento, undrained
2 tablespoons olive or vegetable oil
1 tablespoon water
1 teaspoon sugar
¼ teaspoon pepper
1 (6-ounce) head oak leaf or Bibb lettuce
3 ounces curly leaf lettuce leaves
4 small heads Belgian endive, separated into leaves

Combine first 6 ingredients in a small jar. Cover tightly, and shake vigorously. Chill dressing thoroughly.

Arrange lettuce leaves on individual salad plates. Stir dressing, and drizzle 1 tablespoon over each salad before serving. Yield: 10 servings (35 calories per serving).

PROTEIN 0.6 / FAT 2.8 / CARBOHYDRATE 2.0 / FIBER 0.4 / CHOLESTEROL 0 / SODIUM 8 / POTASSIUM 137

MARINATED VEGETABLE SALAD

¼ pound fresh snow peas
4 cherry tomatoes, cut in half
1 medium carrot, scraped and thinly sliced diagonally
½ medium zucchini, thinly sliced diagonally
2 tablespoons vinegar
1 tablespoon vegetable oil
1½ teaspoons sugar
Dash of celery seeds
Dash of dry mustard
Dash of paprika
1 tablespoon feta cheese, crumbled

Cook snow peas in a vegetable steamer over boiling water 3 to 5 minutes or until crisp-tender. Cover and chill thoroughly.

Combine tomatoes, carrot, and zucchini in a 10- x 6- x 2-inch baking dish. Combine vinegar, vegetable oil, sugar, celery seeds, mustard, and paprika in a glass jar; cover tightly, and shake vigorously. Pour over vegetables; cover and marinate 8 hours or overnight in refrigerator, stirring occasionally.

To serve, arrange chilled snow peas on a serving platter; spoon marinated vegetables over top, using a slotted spoon. Sprinkle feta cheese over vegetables. Yield: 2 servings (136 calories per serving).

PROTEIN 3.3 / FAT 7.9 / CARBOHYDRATE 14.6 / FIBER 2.1 / CHOLESTEROL 3 / SODIUM 58 / POTASSIUM 416

CARROT-FRUIT SALAD

2 medium oranges, peeled, sectioned, and seeded
2 medium carrots, grated
1 medium-size Red Delicious apple, chopped
½ stalk celery, thinly sliced
¼ cup seedless raisins
2 tablespoons reduced-calorie mayonnaise
½ teaspoon lemon juice
Leaf lettuce

Combine first 5 ingredients in a medium bowl; toss lightly. Add mayonnaise and lemon juice, stirring until well blended. Chill mixture until serving time.

To serve, spoon mixture onto a lettuce-lined serving platter. Yield: 4 servings (112 calories per serving).

PROTEIN 1.3 / FAT 2.4 / CARBOHYDRATE 23.8 / FIBER 3.3 / CHOLESTEROL 2 / SODIUM 76 / POTASSIUM 363

TOMATO-MOZZARELLA SALAD

4 medium tomatoes, cut into ¼-inch-thick slices
½ medium-size red onion, thinly sliced
2 tablespoons olive oil
2 tablespoons white wine vinegar
¼ teaspoon pepper
20 fresh basil leaves
½ pound part-skim mozzarella cheese, cut into
    ⅛-inch-thick slices

Arrange tomato and onion slices in a shallow baking dish. Combine olive oil, vinegar, and pepper; spoon over tomatoes and onion. Cover and chill 1 hour or until serving time.

Place basil leaves on a serving platter. Arrange tomato, onion, and cheese slices on basil leaves. Spoon any remaining oil and vinegar mixture over tomatoes. Yield: 4 servings (207 calories per serving).

PROTEIN 15.3 / FAT 12.8 / CARBOHYDRATE 9.0 / FIBER 1.4 / CHOLESTEROL 33 / SODIUM 275 / POTASSIUM 379

MUSTARD POTATO SALAD

½ cup reduced-calorie salad dressing
2 tablespoons Dijon mustard
2 tablespoons sweet pickle relish
1 tablespoon white wine vinegar
¼ teaspoon salt
⅛ teaspoon pepper
5 cups cooked, sliced new potatoes
¼ cup minced fresh chives or parsley

Combine first 6 ingredients in a large bowl. Add potatoes, and toss to coat. Cover and chill overnight. Garnish with chives. Yield: 10 servings (92 calories per ½-cup serving).

PROTEIN 1.5 / FAT 1.9 / CARBOHYDRATE 17.5 / FIBER 0.4 / CHOLESTEROL 6 / SODIUM 188 / POTASSIUM 270

RED CABBAGE AND APPLE SLAW

1 cup chopped Granny Smith apple
2 cups chopped or shredded red cabbage
2 tablespoons chopped walnuts, toasted
2 tablespoons raisins
½ cup plain low-fat yogurt
¼ cup unsweetened apple juice
1 tablespoon honey
½ teaspoon ground cinnamon
1 teaspoon poppy seeds

Combine first 4 ingredients in a large bowl; set aside. Combine yogurt, apple juice, honey, and cinnamon in a small bowl, mixing well. Pour dressing over salad, and toss well. Sprinkle with poppy seeds; cover and chill. Yield: 7 servings (61 calories per ½-cup serving).

PROTEIN 1.9 / FAT 1.9 / CARBOHYDRATE 10.4 / FIBER 1.0 / CHOLESTEROL 1 / SODIUM 15 / POTASSIUM 142

TANGERINE–BELGIAN ENDIVE SALAD

⅓ cup unsweetened tangerine juice or orange juice
½ teaspoon cornstarch
4 tangerines, peeled, sectioned, and seeded
½ pound Belgian endive, cut into julienne strips
1 cup watercress leaves
1½ cups sliced fresh mushrooms
4 lettuce leaves
Freshly ground black pepper (optional)

Combine tangerine juice and cornstarch in a small saucepan; bring to a boil. Reduce heat, and simmer until thickened, stirring frequently. Cool; set aside.

Combine tangerines, endive, watercress, and mushrooms in a large bowl. Pour dressing over salad, and toss gently. Chill. Spoon onto lettuce leaves; sprinkle with pepper, if desired. Yield: 4 servings (68 calories per 1-cup serving).

PROTEIN 2.3 / FAT 0.5 / CARBOHYDRATE 15.7 / FIBER 1.3 / CHOLESTEROL 0 / SODIUM 20 / POTASSIUM 506

MANDARIN-BIBB SALAD

1 medium head Bibb lettuce
1 (11-ounce) can unsweetened mandarin oranges, chilled
  and drained
3 tablespoons pecan halves, toasted
2 green onions, thinly sliced
¼ cup Italian reduced-calorie salad dressing

Arrange lettuce, oranges, pecan halves, and green onion on
individual serving plates. Spoon salad dressing over salads. Yield:
4 servings (74 calories per 1-cup serving).

PROTEIN 1.2 / FAT 5.0 / CARBOHYDRATE 9.1 / FIBER 1.0 / CHOLESTEROL 1 / SODIUM 128 /
POTASSIUM 282

LEEK-MUSHROOM SALAD

8 medium leeks, trimmed
2 heads Bibb lettuce, washed and separated
4 medium tomatoes, sliced
8 mushrooms, thinly sliced
Salad Dressing (recipe follows)
2 tablespoons chopped fresh parsley

Place leeks in a large saucepan; add water to cover. Bring to a boil. Cover, reduce heat, and simmer 5 minutes or until tender. Drain; cover and chill. Cut leeks in half lengthwise. Line chilled salad plates with lettuce; top with leeks, tomatoes, and mushrooms. Spoon 1½ tablespoons salad dressing over each salad; garnish with parsley. Yield: 8 servings (155 calories per serving).

Salad Dressing:

¼ cup white wine vinegar
¼ cup olive oil
1 tablespoon Dijon mustard
1 tablespoon water
½ teaspoon sugar
⅛ teaspoon pepper
1 shallot, chopped

Combine all ingredients in container of an electric blender; process until smooth. Cover and chill thoroughly. Yield: ¾ cup.

PROTEIN 3.0 / FAT 7.5 / CARBOHYDRATE 21.1 / FIBER 2.3 / CHOLESTEROL 0 / SODIUM 88 / POTASSIUM 464

MARINATED PEPPER SLAW

1 small head cabbage (about 1½ pounds), shredded
3 medium-size sweet red peppers, seeded and thinly
  sliced
1 medium onion, grated
½ cup white wine vinegar
¼ cup reduced-calorie mayonnaise
1 tablespoon Dijon mustard
1 tablespoon sugar
1 clove garlic, minced
1 teaspoon celery seeds
½ teaspoon salt
½ teaspoon pepper
⅓ cup finely chopped fresh parsley

Combine cabbage, red pepper, and onion in a large bowl; mix well. Set aside.

Combine next 8 ingredients in container of an electric blender; process until smooth. Pour over cabbage; mix well. Cover; chill overnight, tossing occasionally. Add parsley; toss well. Yield 10 servings (54 calories per serving).

PROTEIN 1.4 / FAT 2.1 / CARBOHYDRATE 8.3 / FIBER 1.3 / CHOLESTEROL 2 / SODIUM 222 / POTASSIUM 267

ESCAROLE SALAD

1 (¾-pound) head escarole, torn
2 medium oranges, peeled, seeded, and sectioned
1 small cucumber, thinly sliced
¼ cup unsweetened orange juice
3 tablespoon water
2 tablespoons cider vinegar
1 tablespoon lemon juice
1 tablespoon minced shallot
1 teaspoon poppy seeds
1 teaspoon honey
⅛ teaspoon salt
⅛ teaspoon pepper
¼ cup chopped walnuts

Combine escarole, orange sections, and cucumber in a large bowl; toss gently.

Combine orange juice, water, cider vinegar, lemon juice, shallot, poppy seeds, honey, salt, and pepper in container of an electric blender. Process until well blended. Pour dressing over salad; toss gently. Sprinkle with walnuts. Transfer to individual salad plates to serve. Yield: 6 servings (85 calories per serving).

PROTEIN 2.9 / FAT 3.4 / CARBOHYDRATE 13.0 / FIBER 2.1 / CHOLESTEROL 0 / SODIUM 63 / POTASSIUM 384

LENTIL AND BROWN RICE SALAD

1 cup dry lentils
5 cups water, divided
½ cup brown rice, uncooked
¼ pound cherry tomatoes, halved
¼ cup chopped green onion
3 tablespoons cider vinegar
2 tablespoons peanut oil
2 teaspoons honey
½ teaspoon dried whole oregano

Soak lentils in water to cover in a bowl overnight. Drain. Combine lentils and 4 cups water in a large saucepan; bring to a boil. Cover; reduce heat, and simmer 30 minutes. Drain well, and cool.

Combine brown rice and remaining 1 cup water in a saucepan; bring to a boil. Cover; reduce heat, and simmer 50 minutes or until liquid is absorbed. Remove from heat, and cool.

Combine lentils, rice, and remaining ingredients in a large bowl. Cover and chill. Yield: 4 servings (325 calories per serving).

PROTEIN 13.8 / FAT 7.8 / CARBOHYDRATE 51.9 / FIBER 4.0 / CHOLESTEROL 0 / SODIUM 19 / POTASSIUM 514

MARINATED BLACK-EYED PEA SALAD

1 (10-ounce) package frozen black-eyed peas
1 small head cauliflower (about ¾ pound)
½ cup chopped onion
¼ cup chopped green pepper
1 (2-ounce) jar sliced pimiento, drained
½ cup unsweetened apple juice
½ cup cider vinegar
½ teaspoon dried whole oregano
¼ teaspoon salt
¼ teaspoon pepper
⅛ teaspoon hot sauce
1 clove garlic, crushed

Cook peas according to package directions, omitting salt and fat; drain well. Set aside.

Break cauliflower into flowerets; place in a steaming rack over boiling water. Cover and steam 8 to 10 minutes or until crisp-tender.

Combine prepared vegetables, onion, green pepper, and pimiento. Combine remaining ingredients in a glass jar; cover tightly, and shake vigorously. Pour over vegetables. Cover and refrigerate 8 hours or overnight, stirring occasionally. Yield: 10 servings (61 calories per ½-cup serving).

PROTEIN 3.4 / FAT 0.3 / CARBOHYDRATE 12.2 / FIBER 0.9 / CHOLESTEROL 0 / SODIUM 68 / POTASSIUM 304

GARBANZO-PASTA SALAD

4 ounces spinach fusilli or corkscrew pasta, uncooked
1 (15-ounce) can garbanzo beans, drained
½ cup chopped celery
⅓ cup chopped sweet red pepper
⅓ cup shredded carrot
2 tablespoons chopped fresh chives
3 tablespoons white wine vinegar
2 tablespoons reduced-calorie mayonnaise
1 tablespoon olive or vegetable oil
2 teaspoons Dijon mustard
¼ teaspoon salt
¼ teaspoon pepper
4 medium-size leaves romaine lettuce (optional)
1 medium tomato, cut into wedges

Cook pasta according to package directions, omitting salt. Drain and cool.

Rinse garbanzo beans in a colander under cold running water 1 minute; set colander aside to let beans drain 1 minute.

Combine pasta, beans, celery, red pepper, carrot, and chives in a large bowl; toss lightly to mix well.

Combine vinegar, mayonnaise, olive oil, mustard, salt, and pepper in a small bowl; beat with a wire whisk until well blended. Pour over salad, and toss lightly to coat well. Cover and chill thoroughly.

Serve chilled salad on individual lettuce-lined plates, if desired. Arrange tomato wedges around each serving. Yield: 4 servings (200 calories per serving).

PROTEIN 6.6 / FAT 8.5 / CARBOHYDRATE 24.3 / FIBER 5.3 / CHOLESTEROL 41 / SODIUM 459 / POTASSIUM 450

CURRIED BEAN AND RICE SALAD

1 pound fresh green beans
1 cup water
1 teaspoon chicken-flavored bouillon granules
½ cup parboiled rice, uncooked
½ cup chopped onion
2 tablespoons slivered almonds, toasted
3 tablespoons white wine vinegar
1 tablespoon vegetable oil
1 teaspoon lemon juice
½ teaspoon curry powder
½ teaspoon prepared mustard
⅛ teaspoon pepper

Remove strings from beans; wash beans thoroughly, and cut into 1½-inch pieces. Place beans and water to cover in a medium saucepan. Bring to a boil. Cover; reduce heat, and simmer 10 minutes or until beans are crisp-tender; drain and cool.

Combine 1 cup water and bouillon granules in a small saucepan. Bring to a boil, and stir in rice. Cover; reduce heat, and simmer 20 minutes or until rice is tender. Cool.

Combine beans, rice, onion, and almonds in a medium bowl. Combine remaining ingredients in a jar. Cover tightly, and shake vigorously. Pour over bean mixture; toss gently. Cover and refrigerate overnight. Yield: 10 servings (74 calories per ½-cup serving).

PROTEIN 1.9 / FAT 2.4 / CARBOHYDRATE 11.8 / FIBER 1.3 / CHOLESTEROL 0 / SODIUM 45 / POTASSIUM 134

LAYERED PASTA SALAD

6 ounces multicolored fusilli pasta, uncooked
½ cup red wine vinegar
3 tablespoons grated Parmesan cheese
3 tablespoons olive oil
2 tablespoons dried whole basil
1 tablespoon dried chervil
1 tablespoon water
2 teaspoons garlic powder
5 ounces fresh spinach, shredded
1 cup sliced fresh mushrooms
2 medium tomatoes, seeded and chopped
¾ cup chopped celery
½ cup chopped green onions
3 tablespoons chopped fresh parsley

Cook pasta according to package directions, omitting salt; drain, and set aside. Combine vinegar and next 6 ingredients, stirring well. Pour ½ cup vinegar mixture over reserved cooked pasta. Toss gently. Set aside remaining vinegar mixture.

Layer reserved cooked pasta, spinach, mushrooms, tomatoes, celery, green onions, and parsley in order listed in a large salad bowl. Pour remaining vinegar mixture over salad. (Do not toss.) Cover salad and chill 2 hours. Yield: 10 servings (125 calories per serving).

PROTEIN 3.9 / FAT 4.9 / CARBOHYDRATE 16.5 / CHOLESTEROL 1 / IRON 1.5 / SODIUM 52 / CALCIUM 60

BLACK-AND-WHITE BEAN SALAD

7 ounces dried black beans
7 ounces dried Great Northern beans
1 cup sliced green onions
1 cup diced sweet red pepper
1 cup diced green pepper
1¾ cups peeled, seeded, and chopped tomato
3 tablespoons red wine vinegar
2 tablespoons canned no-salt-added chicken broth, undiluted
1 tablespoon olive oil
1 teaspoon salt
1 clove garlic, minced
½ teaspoon freshly ground pepper

Sort and wash beans; place in separate large Dutch ovens. Cover with water 3 inches above beans. Bring to a boil; boil 5 minutes. Remove from heat. Cover and let stand 1 hour. Drain; return beans to Dutch ovens. Cover with water 3 inches above beans. Bring to a boil. Reduce heat, and simmer 1 hour or until beans are tender. Drain; rinse with cold water. Drain again.

Combine beans, green onions, red pepper, green pepper, and tomato in a serving bowl. Combine vinegar and remaining ingredients, stirring with a wire whisk until well blended. Pour over bean mixture; toss gently. Cover and marinate in refrigerator at least 4 hours. Yield: 16 servings (102 calories per ½-cup serving).

PROTEIN 5.8 / FAT 1.3 / CARBOHYDRATE 17.9 / CHOLESTEROL 0 / IRON 2.1 / SODIUM 152 / CALCIUM 45

CRUNCHY BROWN RICE SALAD

1 cup frozen English peas
2 cups cooked brown rice (cooked without salt or fat)
1 cup diced tomato
1 cup shredded carrot
½ cup diced Jerusalem artichokes
½ cup fresh bean sprouts, washed and drained
½ cup sliced green onions
¼ cup crumbled blue cheese
1 tablespoon plus 1½ teaspoons lemon juice
1 tablespoon vegetable oil
2 teaspoons Dijon mustard
½ teaspoon sugar
¼ teaspoon salt
¼ teaspoon ground white pepper
⅛ teaspoon ground red pepper

Cook peas according to package directions, omitting salt and fat. Drain. Combine peas, rice, and next 6 ingredients in a large bowl. Set aside.

Combine lemon juice and remaining ingredients in a jar; cover tightly and shake vigorously. Pour over rice mixture, and toss well. Cover and chill 3 hours. Yield: 10 servings (93 calories per ½-cup serving).

PROTEIN 2.8 / FAT 2.6 / CARBOHYDRATE 14.9 / CHOLESTEROL 2 / IRON 0.9 / SODIUM 151 / CALCIUM 31

GARDEN TABBOULEH

¾ cup bulgur wheat
1½ cups hot water
3 tablespoons white wine vinegar
2 tablespoons sliced green onions
2 tablespoons sliced radishes
2 tablespoons chopped carrots
2 tablespoons chopped zucchini
1½ teaspoons vegetable oil
¼ teaspoon salt
1 medium tomato, chopped
2 tablespoons chopped fresh parsley
6 lettuce leaves

Place bulgur in a medium-size bowl; add the hot water, and let stand 1 hour. Drain well. Stir in vinegar and next 6 ingredients. Cover and chill thoroughly. Before serving, stir in chopped tomato and parsley. Serve on lettuce leaves. Yield: 6 servings (96 calories per serving).

PROTEIN 2.9 / FAT 1.6 / CARBOHYDRATE 18.2 / CHOLESTEROL 0 / IRON 1.1 / SODIUM 105 / CALCIUM 16

CORN SALAD

2 cups frozen whole kernel corn
1 (4-ounce) jar diced pimiento, drained
½ cup chopped green pepper
¼ cup chopped green onion
1 tablespoon sugar
2 tablespoons cider vinegar
1 tablespoon vegetable oil
1 teaspoon celery seeds
¼ teaspoon salt

Cook corn according to package directions, omitting salt and fat. Drain and cool. Combine corn and remaining ingredients; cover and chill. Yield: 4 servings (133 calories per ½-cup serving).

PROTEIN 3.0 / FAT 4.4 / CARBOHYDRATE 23.5 / FIBER 2.3 / CHOLESTEROL 0 / SODIUM 155 / POTASSIUM 279

HOMINY SALAD

1 (15½-ounce) can golden hominy, drained
¼ cup sliced green onions
3 tablespoons red wine vinegar
3 tablespoons water
1 tablespoon vegetable oil
¼ teaspoon salt
¼ teaspoon pepper
2 cups torn iceberg lettuce
1 cup sliced celery
¼ cup sliced pimiento
2 tablespoons sliced ripe olives

Combine first 7 ingredients in a large bowl, stirring well. Cover and chill 2 hours. Add lettuce, celery, pimiento, and olives just before serving; toss gently. Yield: 6 servings (65 calories per serving).

PROTEIN 1.0 / FAT 3.1 / CARBOHYDRATE 8.4 / CHOLESTEROL 0 / IRON 0.6 / SODIUM 254 / CALCIUM 20

MEXICAN BEAN SALAD

1 (16-ounce) can no-salt-added cut green beans, drained
1 (16-ounce) can wax beans, drained
1 (16-ounce) can kidney beans, rinsed and drained
1 (17-ounce) can no-salt-added whole kernel corn, drained
1 (4-ounce) can diced green chiles, drained
1 medium tomato, diced
½ cup thinly sliced green onions
2 tablespoons minced fresh parsley
2 tablespoons minced fresh cilantro
2 tablespoons vegetable oil
3 tablespoons red wine vinegar
2 teaspoons chili powder
1 teaspoon garlic powder
½ teaspoon hot sauce
¼ teaspoon pepper

Combine first 9 ingredients in a large bowl; toss gently.

Combine oil, red wine vinegar, chili powder, garlic powder, hot sauce, and pepper in a jar; cover tightly, and shake vigorously. Pour over bean mixture, and toss gently. Cover and chill 8 hours. Yield: 16 servings (65 calories per ½-cup serving).

PROTEIN 2.6 / FAT 1.9 / CARBOHYDRATE 10.6 / CHOLESTEROL 0 / IRON 1.1 / SODIUM 62 / CALCIUM 21

MAIN DISH SALADS

Meatless

VEGETARIAN CHEF SALAD

¼ cup reduced-calorie mayonnaise
¼ cup plain nonfat yogurt
2 tablespoons white wine vinegar
1 teaspoon dry mustard
¼ teaspoon sugar
¼ teaspoon salt
¼ teaspoon pepper
2 cups hot cooked brown rice (cooked without salt or fat)
1 pound fresh broccoli
½ pound fresh mushrooms, sliced
1 medium tomato, seeded and chopped
¾ cup coarsely grated carrot
4 ounces Swiss cheese, cut into julienne strips
4 ounces Cheddar cheese, cut into cubes

Combine first 7 ingredients, stirring well. Pour over hot cooked rice in a large bowl; stir well, and set aside to cool.

Trim off large leaves of broccoli; remove stalks, and reserve for use in other recipes. Place broccoli flowerets in a vegetable steamer. Place steamer over boiling water. Cover and steam 5 minutes or until crisp-tender.

Add broccoli, mushrooms, tomato, carrot, and cheeses to reserved rice mixture; toss gently to mix thoroughly. Cover and chill at least 2 hours. Yield: 8 servings (209 calories per serving).

PROTEIN 10.7 / FAT 11.2 / CARBOHYDRATE 17.2 / CHOLESTEROL 31 / IRON 1.0 / SODIUM 273 / CALCIUM 276

MEXICAN SALAD BOWL

1 (15-ounce) can kidney beans
4 ounces sharp Cheddar cheese, diced
1 (8¾-ounce) can whole kernel corn, drained
2 medium tomatoes, diced
½ cup chopped green pepper
4 green onions, thinly sliced
½ cup reduced-calorie French salad dressing
½ to ¾ teaspoon chili powder
1 medium head iceberg lettuce, shredded

Place kidney beans in a colander, and rinse under cold water 1 minute; set colander aside to let beans drain 1 minute.

Combine beans with next 5 ingredients in a large salad bowl. Combine salad dressing and chili powder; pour over bean mixture, tossing gently. Cover and refrigerate 1 hour. Add lettuce just before serving; toss lightly. Yield: 5 servings (205 calories per serving).

PROTEIN 11.5 / FAT 8.6 / CARBOHYDRATE 22.8 / FIBER 7.3 / CHOLESTEROL 24 / SODIUM 516 / POTASSIUM 592

MEATLESS MAIN DISH PEA SALAD

1 (16-ounce) package small frozen English peas, thawed
    and drained
1 small head cauliflower, broken into flowerets
4 green onions, thinly sliced
1 (8-ounce) can sliced water chestnuts, drained
1 sweet red pepper, cut into julienne strips
2½ ounces Swiss cheese, cut into thin strips
3 hard-cooked eggs, chopped
½ cup reduced-calorie mayonnaise
¼ cup reduced-calorie buttermilk salad dressing
1 tablespoon grated Parmesan cheese
1 teaspoon lemon juice
Lettuce leaves

Combine peas, cauliflower, green onions, water chestnuts, red
pepper, Swiss cheese, and eggs in a large bowl, tossing gently.
Combine mayonnaise, salad dressing, Parmesan cheese, and
lemon juice in a small bowl; stir until well blended. Pour mayonnaise mixture over vegetable mixture, tossing gently. Cover salad
and refrigerate 8 hours or overnight. To serve, spoon salad onto
lettuce leaves. Yield: 6 servings (263 calories per serving).

PROTEIN 12.7 / FAT 15.0 / CARBOHYDRATE 23.5 / CHOLESTEROL 158 / IRON 2.7 /
SODIUM 413 / CALCIUM 183

Seafood

CREAMY SHRIMP-ASPARAGUS SALAD

6 ounces bow-tie pasta, uncooked
½ pound fresh asparagus spears
½ cup plain low-fat yogurt
⅓ cup reduced-calorie creamy Italian dressing
1 clove garlic, minced
2 pounds large fresh shrimp, peeled and deveined
12 cherry tomatoes, halved
1 medium cucumber, sliced
1 cup shredded carrot
2 green onions, chopped

Cook bow-tie pasta according to package directions, omitting salt and fat; drain. Rinse with cold water; drain.

Snap off tough ends of asparagus. Remove scales using a knife or vegetable peeler, if desired. Cut asparagus into 1-inch pieces. Cook asparagus, covered, in a small amount of boiling water 2 minutes or until crisp-tender. Drain.

Combine yogurt, dressing, and garlic; stir well. Combine pasta, asparagus, and dressing mixture in a large bowl; toss gently. Set aside.

Bring 1½ quarts water to a boil; add shrimp, and cook 3 to 5 minutes. Drain well; rinse with cold water, and drain again. Add shrimp to reserved pasta mixture. Stir in cherry tomatoes, cucumber, carrot, and green onions. Cover and chill thoroughly. Yield: 12 servings (126 calories per 1-cup serving).

PROTEIN 13.4 / FAT 0.9 / CARBOHYDRATE 15.7 / CHOLESTEROL 86 / IRON 1.6 / SODIUM 152 / CALCIUM 68

COLORFUL SALMON-PASTA SALAD

1½ cups tricolor pasta, uncooked
1 (15½-ounce) can salmon, drained and flaked
¼ cup chopped green pepper
4 green onions, chopped
2 medium carrots, scraped and thinly sliced
1 small zucchini, thinly sliced
3 tablespoons white wine Worcestershire sauce
⅓ cup reduced-calorie mayonnaise
Lettuce leaves

Cook pasta according to package directions, omitting salt and fat; drain. Rinse with cold water; drain. Combine pasta, salmon, and next 4 ingredients; toss gently. Combine Worcestershire sauce and mayonnaise; stir well. Pour over pasta; toss gently. Spoon onto a lettuce-lined serving platter. Yield: 6 servings (239 calories per 1-cup serving).

PROTEIN 17.6 / FAT 10.7 / CARBOHYDRATE 17.0 / CHOLESTEROL 30 / IRON 1.8 / SODIUM 227 / CALCIUM 218

SALADE NIÇOISE

1 (6½-ounce) can water-packed white tuna
½ cup reduced-calorie Italian salad dressing
2 teaspoons dried whole tarragon
4 small new potatoes, unpeeled
2 tablespoons Chablis or other dry white wine
1 clove garlic, crushed
½ pound fresh green beans
4 cups torn Bibb lettuce
½ small purple onion
1 large tomato, cut into wedges
1 hard-cooked egg, sliced
4 pitted ripe olives, sliced in half lengthwise

Place tuna in a colander, and rinse under cold water 1 minute; set colander aside to let tuna drain 1 minute.

Combine dressing and tarragon; stir well, and set aside.

Arrange potatoes in a vegetable steamer. Place over boiling water in a saucepan. Cover and steam 15 minutes or until potatoes are tender. Set aside to cool. Slice cooled potatoes, and combine with wine and garlic. Toss gently. Cover and chill 2 hours.

Wash beans; trim ends, and remove strings. Cook beans, covered, in a small amount of boiling water 5 minutes or until crisp-tender; drain. Combine beans and ¼ cup reserved dressing mixture. Toss gently; cover, and chill 30 minutes.

Place lettuce on 4 serving plates. Cut onion into thin slices; separate into rings. Arrange onion over lettuce. Drain chilled potatoes, discarding liquid. Arrange over onion slices. Drain chilled beans, discarding liquid. Arrange beans, tomato wedges, reserved tuna, egg, and olives on top of onions. Pour remaining reserved dressing mixture evenly over salads. Yield: 4 servings (243 calories per serving).

PROTEIN 16.6 / FAT 3.0 / CARBOHYDRATE 38.4 / CHOLESTEROL 89 / IRON 4.1 / SODIUM 397 / CALCIUM 74

HOT SEAFOOD SALAD

1 quart water
¾ pound fresh medium-size shrimp, unpeeled
¾ pound lump crabmeat, drained and flaked
3 medium stalks celery, thinly sliced
¼ cup chopped sweet red pepper
¼ cup reduced-calorie mayonnaise
2 tablespoons grated onion
1 tablespoon lemon juice
1 tablespoon Worcestershire sauce
2 teaspoons creole mustard
⅛ teaspoon red pepper
Vegetable cooking spray
2 tablespoons grated Parmesan cheese
Fresh parsley sprigs

Bring water to a boil; add shrimp, and reduce heat. Cook 3 minutes. Drain well; rinse with cold water. Let shrimp cool; peel and devein. Cut each shrimp in half.

Combine cooked shrimp and next 3 ingredients in a bowl; stir well. Combine mayonnaise, onion, lemon juice, Worcestershire sauce, mustard, and red pepper in a small bowl. Add to shrimp mixture; stir until well blended.

Spoon shrimp mixture into 6 baking shells or 6-ounce custard cups coated with cooking spray. Sprinkle 1 teaspoon Parmesan cheese over each. Bake at 350° for 15 minutes or until thoroughly heated. Garnish with parsley. Yield: 6 main-dish servings (137 calories each).

PROTEIN 18.7 / FAT 4.8 / CARBOHYDRATE 3.9 / FIBER 0.3 / CHOLESTEROL 125 / SODIUM 342 / POTASSIUM 303

SHRIMP-ASPARAGUS SALAD

1½ quarts water
2 pounds fresh, medium size shrimp, unpeeled
1½ pound fresh asparagus
1 cup shelled fresh English peas
1 pound Boston lettuce, separated into leaves
6 medium carrots, scraped and thinly sliced
1 cup yellow pepper, cut into julienne strips
2 cups thinly sliced cucumber
¼ cup plus 2 tablespoons catsup
¼ cup plus 2 tablespoons reduced-calorie mayonnaise
¼ cup minced dill pickle
¼ cup skim milk

Bring water to a boil in a large saucepan; add shrimp, and reduce heat. Simmer 3 minutes. Drain and rinse with cold water. Peel and devein shrimp. Set shrimp aside in refrigerator.

Snap off tough ends of asparagus. Remove scales from stalks, if desired, using a knife or vegetable peeler. Cook asparagus, covered, in a small amount of boiling water 6 to 8 minutes or until crisp-tender; drain and chill. Cook peas, covered, in boiling water to cover 6 to 8 minutes or until crisp-tender; drain and chill.

Place lettuce leaves on 8 individual plates; arrange shrimp, asparagus, peas, carrots, yellow pepper, and cucumber on lettuce.

Combine catsup, mayonnaise, pickle, and skim milk in a small bowl, mixing well. Spoon 2 tablespoons dressing over each salad to serve. Yield: 8 servings (196 calories per serving).

PROTEIN 21.0 / FAT 4.3 / CARBOHYDRATE 19.8 / FIBER 3.4 / CHOLESTEROL 131 / SODIUM 470 / POTASSIUM 899

SHRIMP SALAD IN TOMATO CUPS

1½ pounds fresh medium-size shrimp, unpeeled
2 tablespoons olive oil
¼ cup dry white wine
1 teaspoon lemon juice
1 (0.6-ounce) envelope Italian salad dressing mix
Dash of pepper
1 cup frozen English peas, cooked and drained
3 tablespoons sliced green onion
6 medium tomatoes

Add shrimp to boiling water, and reduce heat. Simmer 3 minutes. Drain well, and chill. Peel and devein shrimp; set aside.

Combine olive oil, wine, lemon juice, salad dressing mix, and pepper in a jar. Cover tightly, and shake vigorously.

Combine shrimp, peas, and green onion. Pour dressing over shrimp mixture; toss to coat well. Cover and chill at least 2 hours.

Cut tops from tomatoes; scoop out pulp, leaving shells intact. Reserve pulp for use in another recipe. Invert tomato shells on paper towels, and allow to drain.

Drain shrimp mixture, and spoon into tomato cups. Yield: 6 servings (161 calories per serving).

Note: Frozen shrimp may be substituted for fresh shrimp.

PROTEIN 17.6 / FAT 5.4 / CARBOHYDRATE 9.8 / FIBER 0.7 / CHOLESTEROL 128 / SODIUM 511 / POTASSIUM 367

MARINATED CRAB SALAD

1 pound fresh crabmeat, drained and flaked
½ cup chopped onion
2 tablespoons cider vinegar
2 teaspoons Dijon mustard
½ teaspoon minced garlic
½ teaspoon dried whole basil
½ teaspoon lemon juice
¼ teaspoon freshly ground black pepper
4 lettuce leaves

Combine crabmeat and onion in a bowl. Combine next 6 ingredients in a small bowl, and pour over crabmeat mixture. Toss gently to mix well; cover and chill overnight. Spoon onto lettuce leaves to serve. Yield: 4 servings (121 calories per serving).

PROTEIN 20.1 / FAT 2.4 / CARBOHYDRATE 3.5 / FIBER 0.4 / CHOLESTEROL 113 / SODIUM 315 / POTASSIUM 286

Poultry

FESTIVE TURKEY SALAD

3 cups coarsely chopped cooked turkey breast (skinned
   before cooking and cooked without salt)
¼ chopped celery
1 cup chopped Red Delicious apple
¼ cup coarsely chopped pecans
3 tablespoons reduced-calorie mayonnaise
Red leaf lettuce leaves
Cranberry-French Dressing (recipe follows)
Fresh celery leaves (optional)

Combine first 5 ingredients in a large bowl; stir well. Cover and
chill thoroughly. To serve, place 1 cup turkey mixture onto each of
4 lettuce-lined salad plates. Top each serving with 2 tablespoons
Cranberry-French Dressing. Garnish with fresh celery leaves, if
desired. Yield: 4 servings (271 calories each).

Cranberry-French Dressing:

¼ cup jellied cranberry sauce
⅛ teaspoon salt
⅛ teaspoon paprika
⅛ teaspoon dry mustard
⅛ teaspoon pepper
2 tablespoons vinegar
1 tablespoon vegetable oil

Combine first 5 ingredients in a small bowl, stirring with a wire
whisk until smooth. Gradually add vinegar to cranberry mixture
alternately with vegetable oil, beginning and ending with vinegar;
stir well after each addition. Yield: ½ cup.

PROTEIN 26.0 / FAT 14.3 / CARBOHYDRATE 9.0 / CHOLESTEROL 62 / IRON 1.4 / SODIUM 226 /
CALCIUM 26

COBB SALAD

3 cups torn romaine lettuce
2 cups torn curly endive
1 cup torn watercress
2 cups thinly sliced, cooked chicken (skinned before cooking
  and cooked without salt)
1 large tomato, thinly sliced
½ medium avocado
2 hard-cooked eggs, sliced
2 tablespoons plus 2 teaspoons crumbled Roquefort cheese
3 tablespoons plus 2 teaspoons water
2 tablespoons lemon juice
2 tablespoons vegetable oil
1 teaspoon dry mustard
1 teaspoon white wine vinegar
⅛ teaspoon pepper

Combine first 3 ingredients; toss well. Divide salad greens among
4 individual serving plates. Arrange chicken over salad greens.
Arrange tomato, avocado, and egg slices over salads. Sprinkle 2
teaspoons cheese over each salad.

Combine remaining ingredients in a jar; cover tightly, and shake
vigorously. Top each salad with 2 tablespoons dressing. Yield: 4
servings (287 calories per serving).

PROTEIN 22.1 / FAT 18.8 / CARBOHYDRATE 8.5 / CHOLESTEROL 186 / IRON 2.4 / SODIUM 282 /
CALCIUM 140

SPICY CHICKEN SALAD

½ teaspoon pepper
¼ teaspoon paprika
⅛ teaspoon dried whole thyme
⅛ teaspoon celery seeds
Dash of crushed red pepper
6 (4-ounce) boneless chicken breast halves, skinned
Vegetable cooking spray
2 teaspoons vegetable oil
¾ cup chicken broth
¼ cup dry white wine
½ cup thinly sliced green onion
½ cup diced sweet red or green pepper
1 tablespoon plus 1 teaspoon lemon juice
3 cups torn red leaf lettuce
3 cups torn Boston lettuce
3 cups torn spinach leaves
1 cup torn endive

Combine first 5 ingredients; sprinkle over chicken breasts, and set aside. Coat a heavy skillet with cooking spray; add vegetable oil, and place over medium heat until hot. Add chicken, and cook until browned. Add broth and wine, and bring to a boil. Cover; reduce heat to low, and cook 25 minutes or until chicken is done. Transfer chicken to a plate. Cover; set aside, and keep warm.

Pour pan juices into a large bowl. Stir in green onion, red pepper, and lemon juice; add lettuce, spinach, and endive, and toss well.

Divide dressed greens among individual serving plates. Slice chicken breasts into ¼-inch-thick strips, and arrange over greens. Spoon any remaining dressing over chicken. Serve warm. Yield: 6 servings (134 calories per serving).

PROTEIN 19.7 / FAT 4.0 / CARBOHYDRATE 4.9 / FIBER 1.8 / CHOLESTEROL 47 / SODIUM 166 / POTASSIUM 554

LIME CHICKEN SALAD

1 cup fresh parsley sprigs
¼ cup plus 1 tablespoon lime juice
2 tablespoons vegetable oil
1 tablespoon water
2 cloves garlic
1 teaspoon ground cumin
½ teaspoon pepper
2 cups chopped, cooked chicken or turkey breasts
1 medium-size green pepper, seeded and cut into thin
    strips
1 cup thinly sliced red onion
1 cup canned garbanzo beans, rinsed and drained
½ cup diced, peeled avocado

Combine first 7 ingredients in container of an electric blender, and process until smooth; set aside. Combine chicken, green pepper, onion, and garbanzo beans in a bowl; add dressing, and mix well. Add avocado, and toss gently. Chill. Yield: 6 servings (192 calories per 1-cup serving).

PROTEIN 17.7 / FAT 8.2 / CARBOHYDRATE 12.3 / FIBER 3.5 / CHOLESTEROL 40 / SODIUM 207 / POTASSIUM 495

Beef

WARM FAJITA SALAD WITH SALSA

1 (1-pound) lean flank steak
¼ cup Burgundy or other dry red wine
¼ cup lime juice
½ teaspoon garlic powder
½ teaspoon ground cumin
2 cups seeded, diced tomato
1 small green pepper, seeded and diced
1 jalapeño pepper, seeded and diced
2 tablespoons diced purple onion
1 tablespoon minced fresh cilantro
2 teaspoons red wine vinegar
Vegetable cooking spray
6 cups torn romaine lettuce
½ cup (2 ounces) shredded extra-sharp Cheddar cheese

Trim fat from steak, and place in a large shallow dish. Combine red wine, lime juice, garlic powder, and cumin, stirring well; pour over steak. Cover and marinate in refrigerator 24 hours, turning steak occasionally.

Combine tomato and next 5 ingredients, stirring well. Set aside.

Remove steak from marinade; discard marinade. Place steak on rack in a broiler pan that has been coated with cooking spray. Broil steak 4 inches from heating element 12 to 17 minutes or to desired degree of doneness, turning once. Cut diagonally across grain into thin slices. Combine steak, lettuce, and cheese in a large bowl; toss gently. Spoon ⅓ cup salsa mixture over each serving. Serve warm. Yield: 6 servings (210 calories per serving).

PROTEIN 18.8 / FAT 12.2 / CARBOHYDRATE 5.7 / CHOLESTEROL 51 / IRON 2.7 / SODIUM 117 / CALCIUM 100

MARINATED FLANK STEAK SALAD

1 (1-pound) beef flank steak
Vegetable cooking spray
1 medium onion, thinly sliced
1 medium-size green pepper, seeded and cut into thin strips
1 cup sliced fresh mushrooms
1 (2-ounce) jar sliced pimiento, drained
Marinade (recipe follows)
Lettuce leaves
2 medium tomatoes, cut into wedges

Trim excess fat from steak; set steak aside. Coat a broiler rack with cooking spray. Place steak on rack. Broil 3 to 4 inches from heating element 5 to 7 minutes on each side or to desired degree of doneness. Cut steak diagonally across grain into thin slices; cut slices into 1½-inch pieces. Cool slightly.

Combine steak, onion, green pepper, mushrooms, pimiento, and marinade in a shallow container. Cover and refrigerate 8 hours or overnight. Spoon salad into a lettuce-lined serving bowl; garnish with tomato wedges. Yield: 6 main-dish servings (180 calories each).

Marinade:

½ cup red wine vinegar
2 tablespoons Dijon mustard
1 tablespoon olive or vegetable oil
1 tablespoon vegetable oil
1 tablespoon lemon juice
½ teaspoon dried whole basil
¼ teaspoon dried whole thyme
¼ teaspoon salt
¼ teaspoon pepper
1 clove garlic, minced

Combine all ingredients in a small bowl. Stir with a wire whisk until well blended. Yield: about 1 cup.

PROTEIN 19.2 / FAT 8.2 / CARBOHYDRATE 6.3 / FIBER 0.9 / CHOLESTEROL 37 / SODIUM 288 / POTASSIUM 458

STEAK SALAD WITH BLUE CHEESE DRESSING

4 cups watercress leaves
⅓ cup sliced red onion
2 tablespoons chopped fresh parsley
1 tablespoon olive oil
1 tablespoon water
1 tablespoon red wine vinegar
1 clove garlic, minced
⅛ teaspoon pepper
¾ pound lean broiled steak, cut across grain into 2-inch strips
¾ cup sliced radishes
½ cup coarsely crumbled blue cheese

Line a large serving bowl with watercress. Combine next 7 ingredients in a bowl. Add steak and radishes; toss well. Spoon salad over watercress. Sprinkle with blue cheese. Yield: 4 servings (249 calories per serving).

PROTEIN 31.1 / FAT 12.1 / CARBOHYDRATE 2.7 / FIBER 0.5 / CHOLESTEROL 66 / SODIUM 269 / POTASSIUM 545

ORIENTAL BEEF SALAD

¼ teaspoon chicken-flavored bouillon granules
¼ cup warm water (105° to 115°)
2 tablespoons white wine vinegar
2 tablespoons chopped green onion
1 clove garlic, minced
2 teaspoons minced, peeled gingerroot
2 teaspoons reduced-sodium soy sauce
½ teaspoon sugar
⅛ teaspoon pepper
¾ pound lean round steak
2 teaspoons peanut oil
Vegetable cooking spray
¼ pound snow peas
1 teaspoon dry mustard
1 tablespoon hot water
2 tablespoons chopped fresh parsley
2 tablespoons sour cream
1 tablespoon peanut butter
⅛ teaspoon crushed red pepper
4 ounces bean thread noodles or other oriental spaghetti-
   type pasta, uncooked
2 cups boiling water
1 teaspoon sesame seeds, toasted
1 cup coarsely grated carrot
1 medium cucumber, sliced

Combine bouillon granules and the warm water in a 10- x 6- x 2-inch baking dish. Add next 7 ingredients, stirring well; set aside. Trim excess fat from steak; add steak to marinade, turning to coat well. Cover and marinate in refrigerator overnight, turning occasionally.

Remove steak from marinade, reserving marinade; pat dry. Heat peanut oil in a skillet or grill pan coated with cooking spray over medium-high heat until hot. Add steak to skillet; cook 2 minutes on each side for rare meat or to desired degree of

Creamy Shrimp-Asparagus Salad (page 38) is a shrimp-lover's delight.

*The sprightly flavor mix in the Mandarin-Bibb Salad (page 20)
makes it a tasty accompaniment to any entrée.*

Marinated Vegetable Salad (page 14) is a delicious foretaste of things to come.

Poppy Seed Dressing (page 66) (left) is a wonderful accompaniment to fresh fruit salads. A crisp mix of salad greens will leap to life with the addition of Raspberry Vinegar Dressing (page 67) (rear) or chunky Tomatillo Dressing (page 68) spiced with cilantro and chervil.

Salade Niçoise (page 40), a lightened classic from the South of France, is made with water-packed tuna.

Mexican Salad Bowl (page 36) is a protein-rich fiesta of flavor!

Salads offer ideas for more than one course. Serve Tomato-Mozzarella Salad (page 16) to complement the main course. Fruit salads, such as Four Berry Salad (page 60), can make a naturally sweet dessert, and Steak Salad with Blue Cheese Dressing (page 51) is hearty enough for the main course.

Marinated Green Bean Salad (page 11) in the making. The result—a delicious salad with only 43 calories per serving.

Creamy Vegetable Garden Salad Dressing (page 62) has a fresh-from-the-garden flavor.

Warm Fajita Salad with Salsa (page 49) is a spicy, satisfying main-dish salad.

Shrimp Salad in Tomato Cups (page 43) would be center attraction at any luncheon, formal or informal.

Salads provide a wide variety of ingredients for the calorie conscious. Marinated Flank Steak Salad (page 50) can serve as a main dish. For side-dish salads, choose Congealed Apricot-Fruit Salad (page 59) or Fusilli Fruit Salad (page 58).

doneness. Remove meat, reserving pan drippings; slice diagonally across the grain into ¼-inch-thick slices. Set aside; keep warm.

Trim ends of snow peas, and remove strings. Place in a steaming basket. Plunge basket into boiling water, and remove immediately. Place peas in a bowl of ice water to cool quickly. Remove from water, and refrigerate.

Combine mustard and the hot water in a small bowl. Combine mustard mixture, reserved marinade, reserved pan drippings, parsley, sour cream, peanut butter, and red pepper in container of an electric blender; process until smooth. Set sauce aside.

Place noodles in a large bowl; add boiling water, and let stand 10 minutes or until softened. Drain.

Place noodles on a serving platter; sprinkle with sesame seeds. Arrange steak, snow peas, and carrot attractively on noodles. Arrange cucumber around outside edge of platter. Serve with reserved sauce. Yield: 4 servings (369 calories per serving).

PROTEIN 34.1 / FAT 11.6 / CARBOHYDRATE 31.0 / FIBER 2.3 / CHOLESTEROL 58 / SODIUM 210 / POTASSIUM 683

Pork

ZESTY BROCCOLI-HAM SALAD

1¼ pounds fresh broccoli
1½ cups cubed lean cooked ham
½ cup (2 ounces) shredded Swiss cheese
¼ cup chopped sweet red pepper
¼ cup chopped green onion
½ cup reduced-calorie Italian salad dressing
¼ cup cider vinegar
1 tablespoon Dijon mustard
½ teaspoon dried whole savory
⅛ teaspoon freshly ground pepper

Trim off large leaves of broccoli. Remove rough ends of lower stalks. Wash broccoli thoroughly; chop coarsely. Combine broccoli, ham, cheese, red pepper, and green onion in a large serving bowl; toss gently.

Combine remaining ingredients in a small bowl; stir well. Pour over vegetable mixture; toss gently. Cover and refrigerate 8 hours or overnight. Yield: 6 servings (123 calories per serving).

PROTEIN 12.4 / FAT 5.0 / CARBOHYDRATE 8.2 / FIBER 1.3 / CHOLESTEROL 27 / SODIUM 721 / POTASSIUM 39

FRUITED PORK SALAD

1 tablespoon plus 1 teaspoon lime juice
2 teaspoons honey
2 teaspoons olive oil
1 teaspoon water
¼ teaspoon pepper
¼ teaspoon ground coriander
2 cups sliced seedless red grapes
1½ cups cubed roast pork
⅓ cup sliced green onion
4 lettuce leaves

Combine lime juice, honey, olive oil, water, pepper, and coriander in a small bowl.

Combine grapes, pork, and green onion in a large bowl; add dressing, and toss gently. Cover and chill thoroughly to blend flavors. Serve over lettuce leaves. Yield: 4 servings (223 calories per serving).

PROTEIN 14.2 / FAT 10.7 / CARBOHYDRATE 18.8 / FIBER 1.8 / CHOLESTEROL 51 / SODIUM 44 / POTASSIUM 394

FRUIT SALADS

MINTY APPLE-CUCUMBER SALAD

¼ cup plain low-fat yogurt
1 tablespoon lemon juice
1 tablespoon minced fresh mint leaves
1 large cucumber, peeled, seeded, and diced
1 medium Granny Smith apple, cored and cut into
   julienne strips
1 small Red Delicious apple, cored and cut into julienne
   strips
1 tablespoon plus 1½ teaspoons unsalted sunflower
   kernels, toasted

Combine first 3 ingredients in a large bowl; stir well. Cover and chill 1 hour.

   Add cucumber, apple, and sunflower kernels to yogurt mixture; toss gently. Cover and chill thoroughly. Yield: 8 servings (33 calories per ½-cup serving).

PROTEIN 1.0 / FAT 1.1 / CARBOHYDRATE 5.7 / CHOLESTEROL 0 / IRON 0.3 / SODIUM 7 / CALCIUM 23

WALDORF-GRAPE SALAD

3 medium-size Red Delicious apples, cored and cubed
1 cup seedless green grapes, halved
¾ cup chopped celery
⅓ cup reduced-calorie salad dressing
2 teaspoons lemon juice
8 lettuce leaves

Combine first 5 ingredients in a bowl; mix well. Cover and chill at least 1 hour. Serve on lettuce leaves. Yield: 8 servings (62 calories per ½-cup serving).

PROTEIN 0.6 / FAT 1.7 / CARBOHYDRATE 12.5 / FIBER 1.7 / CHOLESTEROL 5 / SODIUM 24 / POTASSIUM 160

FUSILLI FRUIT SALAD

1 cup fusilli pasta, uncooked
1 (8-ounce) can unsweetened pineapple chunks,
  undrained
1 cup cantaloupe chunks
1 cup seedless white grapes, halved
1 (8-ounce) carton peach low-fat yogurt
1 cup strawberry halves
Lettuce leaves

Cook pasta according to package directions, omitting salt; drain
and set aside.

Drain pineapple, reserving 2 tablespoons juice. Combine pasta,
pineapple chunks, cantaloupe, and grapes in a medium bowl; set
aside.

Combine yogurt and reserved 2 tablespoons pineapple juice in a
small bowl; stir well. Spoon over pasta mixture, tossing lightly.
Cover and refrigerate 2 hours.

Stir in strawberry halves, and serve on lettuce leaf-lined plates.
Yield: 8 servings (109 calories per serving).

PROTEIN 3.2 / FAT 0.8 / CARBOHYDRATE 23.3 / FIBER 1.5 / CHOLESTEROL 1 / SODIUM 20 /
POTASSIUM 261

CONGEALED APRICOT-FRUIT SALAD

1 (12-ounce) can apricot nectar
1 envelope unflavored gelatin
1 (15¼-ounce) can unsweetened crushed pineapple,
    undrained
1 tablespoon lemon juice
1 (16-ounce) can unsweetened apricot halves, drained
    and chopped
1 medium banana, chopped
Vegetable cooking spray
Lettuce leaves
Mandarin orange slices (optional)

Combine apricot nectar and gelatin in a small saucepan; let stand 1 minute. Cook over medium heat 1 minute or until gelatin dissolves.

Drain pineapple, reserving ½ cup juice. Stir ½ cup pineapple juice and lemon juice into apricot mixture. Chill until consistency of unbeaten egg white.

Add pineapple, apricots, and banana to gelatin mixture, stirring gently. Spoon mixture into a 4-cup mold coated with cooking spray. Chill overnight or until firm. Turn salad out onto a lettuce-lined serving dish. Garnish with mandarin orange slices, if desired. Yield: 8 servings (84 calories per serving).

PROTEIN 1.8 / FAT 0.4 / CARBOHYDRATE 20.2 / FIBER 1.4 / CHOLESTEROL 0 / SODIUM 3 / POTASSIUM 281

FOUR-BERRY SALAD

1 cup fresh blueberries
1 cup fresh raspberries
1 cup fresh blackberries or dewberries
1 cup sliced fresh strawberries
2 tablespoons slivered almonds, toasted
¼ cup sour cream
½ cup plain low-fat yogurt
1 tablespoon plus 1 teaspoon honey
1 tablespoon cream sherry
1 tablespoon lemon juice

Arrange berries in a large serving bowl, and sprinkle with almonds; set aside. Combine sour cream, yogurt, honey, sherry, and lemon juice in a small bowl. Spoon berries into individual serving bowls, and top with yogurt mixture. Yield: 8 servings (84 calories per ½-cup serving).

PROTEIN 1.9 / FAT 3.1 / CARBOHYDRATE 13.1 / FIBER 2.5 / CHOLESTEROL 4 / SODIUM 16 / POTASSIUM 171

DRESSINGS

GREEN GODDESS DRESSING

1 cup loosely packed fresh parsley
¼ cup minced fresh chives
½ teaspoon dried whole tarragon
1 cup low-fat cottage cheese
⅓ cup skim milk
3 tablespoons lemon juice
1 tablespoon tarragon vinegar
½ teaspoon hot sauce

Combine all ingredients in container of an electric blender or food processor; process until mixture is smooth. Cover and chill dressing at least 1 hour. Serve dressing with salad greens. Yield: 1½ cups (9 calories per tablespoon).

PROTEIN 1.4 / FAT 0.1 / CARBOHYDRATE 0.8 / CHOLESTEROL 0 / IRON 0.2 / SODIUM 42 / CALCIUM 14

VEGETABLE GARDEN SALAD DRESSING

1 (8-ounce) carton plain low-fat yogurt
½ cup low-fat sour cream
¼ cup shredded carrot
¼ cup chopped green onions
¼ cup diced radishes
¼ cup minced fresh parsley
2 tablespoons crumbled blue cheese
¼ teaspoon ground white pepper

Combine all ingredients in a small bowl; stir well. Cover and chill thoroughly. Serve with salad greens. Yield: 2 cups (14 calories per tablespoon).

PROTEIN 0.7 / FAT 0.8 / CARBOHYDRATE 0.9 / CHOLESTEROL 3 / IRON 0.1 / SODIUM 20 / CALCIUM 23

HERBED GARLIC DRESSING

½ cup low-fat sour cream
½ cup plain low-fat yogurt
2 tablespoons white wine vinegar
1 tablespoon minced fresh parsley
2 cloves garlic, minced
½ teaspoon dried whole rosemary, crushed
¼ teaspoon hot sauce
⅛ teaspoon dried whole thyme

Combine all ingredients in a small bowl, stirring well. Cover and chill thoroughly. Serve dressing with salad greens. Yield: 1 cup (16 calories per tablespoon).

PROTEIN 0.6 / FAT 1.0 / CARBOHYDRATE 1.0 / CHOLESTEROL 3 / IRON 0.1 / SODIUM 9 / CALCIUM 22

TANGY SOUR CREAM–HORSERADISH DRESSING

1 tablespoon all-purpose flour
¼ teaspoon salt
⅛ teaspoon ground red pepper
¾ cup skim milk
¼ cup prepared horseradish
2 teaspoons prepared mustard
2 egg yolks, beaten
3 tablespoons lemon juice
¾ cup low-fat sour cream

Combine flour, salt, and red pepper in a heavy saucepan; gradually add skim milk, horseradish, and mustard, stirring until smooth. Cook over low heat until thickened and bubbly, stirring constantly. Remove from heat. Gradually stir about one fourth of hot mixture into yolks; add to remaining hot mixture, stirring constantly. Cook over low heat, stirring constantly, until thickened. Transfer mixture to a small bowl; let cool to room temperature. Stir in lemon juice. Cover and chill thoroughly. Fold sour cream into chilled mixture. Serve with salad greens. Yield: 2¼ cups (14 calories per tablespoon).

PROTEIN 0.5 / FAT 0.9 / CARBOHYDRATE 0.9 / CHOLESTEROL 17 / IRON 0.1 / SODIUM 27 / CALCIUM 14

TOMATO-BASIL VINAIGRETTE

⅔ cup no-salt-added tomato juice
⅓ cup red wine vinegar
2 tablespoons finely minced fresh basil
¼ teaspoon onion powder
⅛ teaspoon salt
⅛ teaspoon garlic powder
3 drops hot sauce

Combine all ingredients in a jar. Cover tightly, and shake vigorously. Chill thoroughly. Shake dressing again before serving. Serve with salad greens. Yield: 1 cup (3 calories per tablespoon).

PROTEIN 0.1 / FAT 0.0 / CARBOHYDRATE 0.6 / CHOLESTEROL 0 / IRON 0.0 / SODIUM 20 / CALCIUM 2

APPLESAUCE-BANANA DRESSING

1 (8-ounce) carton banana low-fat yogurt
½ cup unsweetened applesauce
⅛ teaspoon ground cardamom

Combine all ingredients in container of an electric blender; top with cover, and process until smooth. Cover and chill thoroughly. Serve over fresh fruit. Yield: 1½ cups (12 calories per tablespoon).

PROTEIN 0.4 / FAT 0.1 / CARBOHYDRATE 2.3 / CHOLESTEROL 0 / IRON 0.0 / SODIUM 5 / CALCIUM 13

CREAMY ORANGE-NUTMEG DRESSING

1 (8-ounce) carton plain low-fat yogurt
3 tablespoons unsweetened orange juice
1 tablespoon honey
½ teaspoon grated orange rind
¼ teaspoon ground nutmeg

Combine all ingredients, stirring with a wire whisk until well blended. Cover and chill thoroughly. Serve with fresh fruit. Yield: 1 cup (14 calories per tablespoon).

PROTEIN 0.8 / FAT 0.2 / CARBOHYDRATE 2.4 / CHOLESTEROL 1 / IRON 0.0 / SODIUM 10 / CALCIUM 26

POPPY SEED DRESSING

1 tablespoon cornstarch
1 teaspoon sugar
½ teaspoon dry mustard
1 cup water
3 tablespoons honey
3 tablespoons vinegar
1 tablespoon poppy seeds

Combine cornstarch, sugar, and mustard in a small nonaluminum saucepan. Stir in the water, honey, and vinegar; bring to a boil. Reduce heat to medium, and cook, stirring constantly, until thickened and bubbly. Remove from heat, and cool slightly. Stir in poppy seeds. Cover and chill thoroughly. Serve with fresh fruit. Yield: 1⅓ cups (14 calories per tablespoon).

PROTEIN 0.1 / FAT 0.2 / CARBOHYDRATE 3.2 / CHOLESTEROL 0 / IRON 0.1 / SODIUM 0 / CALCIUM 6

RASPBERRY VINEGAR

1½ cups white wine vinegar
½ cup Chambord or other raspberry-flavored liqueur
2 sprigs fresh dillweed

Combine vinegar and liqueur in a small nonaluminum saucepan; bring to a boil. Reduce heat, and simmer 5 minutes. Let cool.

Place dillweed in a wide-mouth glass jar. Pour vinegar mixture over dillweed, and cover. Let stand at room temperature for 24 hours. Serve with salad greens. Yield: 2 cups (13 calories per tablespoon).

PROTEIN 0.0 / FAT 0.0 / CARBOHYDRATE 1.0 / CHOLESTEROL 0 / IRON 0.0 / SODIUM 1 / CALCIUM 0

RUM FRUIT DRESSING

½ cup pear nectar
1 tablespoon dark rum
1 teaspoon lime juice
¼ teaspoon ground nutmeg

Combine all ingredients, stirring well. Cover and chill thoroughly. Serve with fresh fruit. Yield: ½ cup (13 calories per tablespoon).

PROTEIN 0.1 / FAT 0.1 / CARBOHYDRATE 2.1 / CHOLESTEROL 0 / IRON 0.0 / SODIUM 0 / CALCIUM 1

TOMATILLO DRESSING

½ pound fresh tomatillos
3 tablespoons loosely packed fresh cilantro
1 tablespoon vegetable oil
1 teaspoon dried chervil
¼ teaspoon salt
1 clove garlic
1 teaspoon lime juice

Place tomatillos on a baking sheet; bake at 450° for 10 minutes. Remove from oven; cool. Remove husks, rinse tomatillos.

Position knife blade in food processor bowl; add tomatillos and remaining ingredients. Process until smooth. Cover and chill thoroughly. Serve with lettuce, sliced tomatoes, or cucumbers. Yield: 1 cup (11 calories per tablespoon).

PROTEIN 0.2 / FAT 0.9 / CARBOHYDRATE 0.8 / CHOLESTEROL 0 / IRON 0.1 / SODIUM 38 / CALCIUM 3

TANGY WHITE WINE DRESSING

1 cup water
½ cup white wine vinegar
2 tablespoons plus ¾ teaspoon powdered fruit pectin
2 tablespoons fresh lemon juice
1 green onion, chopped
1 clove garlic, crushed
1 teaspoon sugar
¼ teaspoon dried red pepper flakes, crushed
¼ teaspoon salt
¼ teaspoon white pepper

Combine all ingredients in container of an electric blender; process until smooth. Cover and chill. Stir well before serving over salad greens. Yield: 1¾ cups (5 calories per tablespoon).

PROTEIN 0.0 / FAT 0.0 / CARBOHYDRATE 1.2 / FIBER 0.0 / CHOLESTEROL 0 / SODIUM 22

TARRAGON DRESSING

1 cup low-fat cottage cheese
¼ cup reduced-calorie mayonnaise
¼ cup tarragon vinegar
2 teaspoons sugar
½ teaspoon dried whole tarragon
½ teaspoon dry mustard
⅛ teaspoon salt
⅛ teaspoon pepper
1 tablespoon chopped fresh parsley

Combine first 8 ingredients in container of an electric blender; process until smooth. Stir in parsley. Cover and chill thoroughly. Serve over salad greens. Yield: 1½ cups (17 calories per tablespoon).

PROTEIN 1.3 / FAT 0.9 / CARBOHYDRATE 0.9 / FIBER 0.0 / CHOLESTEROL 2 / SODIUM 69 / POTASSIUM 14

SPRING ONION SALAD DRESSING

1½ cups chopped green onion
½ cup finely chopped onion
1 cup low-fat cottage cheese
1 tablespoon lemon juice
½ teaspoon seasoned salt
⅛ teaspoon pepper

Combine all ingredients in container of an electric blender; process until smooth. Cover and chill thoroughly. Serve over salad greens. Yield: 1¾ cups (10 calories per tablespoon).

PROTEIN 1.2 / FAT 0.2 / CARBOHYDRATE 1.0 / FIBER 0.2 / CHOLESTEROL 1 / SODIUM 64 / POTASSIUM 26

CREAMY PEPPER DRESSING

¾ cup plain low-fat yogurt
¼ cup reduced-calorie mayonnaise
1 tablespoon grated Parmesan cheese
1 tablespoon minced green onion
1½ teaspoons freshly ground pepper
1½ teaspoons cider vinegar
1 teaspoon lemon juice
½ teaspoon Worcestershire sauce

Combine all ingredients in a bowl. Stir with a wire whisk until smooth. Cover; chill thoroughly. Stir well before serving over salad greens. Yield: 1¼ cups (15 calories per tablespoon).

PROTEIN 0.6 / FAT 1.0 / CARBOHYDRATE 1.1 / FIBER 0.0 / CHOLESTEROL 2 / SODIUM 34 / POTASSIUM 27

LEMON-MUSTARD DRESSING

½ cup plain low-fat yogurt
½ cup commercial sour cream
2 tablespoons lemon juice
2 tablespoons white wine vinegar
1 tablespoon chopped fresh parley
1 teaspoon sugar
1 teaspoon dry mustard

Combine all ingredients in a small bowl; stir with a wire whisk until well blended. Cover and chill thoroughly. Serve over salad greens. Yield: 1¼ cups (18 calories per tablespoon).

PROTEIN 0.5 / FAT 1.3 / CARBOHYDRATE 1.0 / FIBER 0.0 / CHOLESTEROL 3 / SODIUM 7 / POTASSIUM 25

CREAMY PINEAPPLE DRESSING

¼ cup sugar
2 tablespoons all-purpose flour
1 cup unsweetened pineapple juice
¼ cup unsweetened orange juice
2 tablespoons lemon juice
1 egg, beaten
¼ teaspoon grated orange rind
½ cup low-fat cottage cheese

Combine sugar and flour in a small nonaluminum saucepan; mix well. Stir in fruit juices. Add egg, mixing until smooth. Cook over low heat, stirring constantly, until thickened. Remove from heat, and stir in orange rind. Chill thoroughly.

Place cottage cheese and ½ cup juice mixture in container of an electric blender; process until smooth. Fold cottage cheese mixture into remaining juice mixture. Serve over fresh fruit. Yield: 2 cups (19 calories per tablespoon).

PROTEIN 0.8 / FAT 0.3 / CARBOHYDRATE 3.5 / FIBER 0.0 / CHOLESTEROL 9 / SODIUM 17 / POTASSIUM 22

HONEY-CURRY DRESSING

½ cup water
2 tablespoons honey
2 teaspoons all-purpose flour
1 teaspoon curry powder
¼ teaspoon dry mustard
⅛ teaspoon salt
1 egg, beaten
2 tablespoons unsweetened orange juice
1 tablespoon vinegar

Combine first 6 ingredients in a nonaluminum saucepan. Add egg; stir well. Add orange juice and vinegar; stir until smooth. Cook over low heat, stirring constantly, until thickened. Cover and chill. Serve over fresh fruit. Yield: 1 cup (16 calories per tablespoon).

PROTEIN 0.5 / FAT 0.4 / CARBOHYDRATE 2.8 / FIBER 0.0 / CHOLESTEROL 17 / SODIUM 23 / POTASSIUM 12

YOGURT-CUCUMBER SALAD DRESSING

1 medium cucumber, peeled, seeded, and finely chopped
⅛ teaspoon salt
1 (16-ounce) carton plain low-fat yogurt
¼ cup thinly sliced green onion
¼ cup chopped green pepper
1 clove garlic, minced
⅛ teaspoon crushed red pepper

Toss cucumber in a bowl with salt. Cover; chill 30 minutes. Rinse and drain cucumber; squeeze out excess moisture with paper towels. Combine cucumber and remaining ingredients in a bowl, mixing well. Cover and refrigerate. Serve over salad greens. Yield: 2¾ cups (8 calories per 1-tablespoon serving).

PROTEIN 0.6 / FAT 0.2 / CARBOHYDRATE 1.0 / FIBER 0.1 / CHOLESTEROL 1 / SODIUM 8 / POTASSIUM 36

THOUSAND ISLAND SALAD DRESSING

1 cup reduced-calorie salad dressing
⅔ cup spicy tomato juice
¼ cup minced dill pickle
1½ tablespoons minced green onion
1½ tablespoons minced green pepper

Combine salad dressing and tomato juice, stirring with a wire whisk until smooth. Stir in remaining ingredients. Cover and refrigerate. Serve over salad greens. Yield: 2 cups (12 calories per 1-tablespoon serving).

PROTEIN 0.1 / FAT 1.0 / CARBOHYDRATE 0.7 / FIBER 0.1 / CHOLESTEROL 4 / SODIUM 53 / POTASSIUM 24

ORANGE–POPPY SEED SALAD DRESSING

1 teaspoon unflavored gelatin
2 cups unsweetened orange juice
1 tablespoon plus 1 teaspoon poppy seeds
2 teaspoons grated orange rind

Combine gelatin and orange juice in a saucepan; let stand 1 minute. Cook over medium heat, stirring constantly, 2 to 3 minutes or until gelatin dissolves. Stir in remaining ingredients; chill overnight. Serve over fruit salads. Yield: 2 cups (9 calories per 1-tablespoon serving).

PROTEIN 0.3 / FAT 0.2 / CARBOHYDRATE 1.8 / FIBER 0.0 / CHOLESTEROL 0 / SODIUM 0 / POTASSIUM 32

CREAMY ONION DRESSING

¾ cup chopped green onions
½ cup plain low-fat yogurt
¼ cup chopped fresh parsley
3 tablespoons white wine vinegar
2 tablespoons reduced-calorie mayonnaise
1 clove garlic, minced
1 teaspoon chopped fresh oregano
½ teaspoon ground white pepper
¼ teaspoon salt

Combine all ingredients in container of an electric blender or food processor; process until smooth. Cover and chill thoroughly. Serve with salad greens. Yield: 1 cup (12 calories per tablespoon).

PROTEIN 0.5 / FAT 0.6 / CARBOHYDRATE 1.1 / CHOLESTEROL 1 / IRON 0.2 / SODIUM 56 / CALCIUM 18

INDEX

Four-berry salad, 60
French-cranberry dressing, 45
Fruit dressing
    applesauce-banana, 65
    orange-nutmeg, creamy, 66
    pineapple, creamy, 71
    rum, 67
Fruited pork salad, 55
Fruit salad
    apple and red cabbage slaw, 18
    apple-cucumber, minty, 56
    apricot, congealed, 59
    cabbage, fruity, 12
    -carrot, 15
    four-berry, 60
    fusilli, 58
    tangerine-Belgian endive, 19
    Waldorf-grape, 57
Fusilli fruit salad, 58

Garbanzo-pasta salad, 26
Garlic
    herbed dressing, 63
    -herb salad, 9
Goat cheese salad, baked Sonoma, 1–2
Grain salad
    tabbouleh, garden, 31
    See also Pasta salad; Rice salad
Grape-Waldorf salad, 57
Green bean salad
    marinated, 11
    See also Bean salad
Green goddess dressing, 61
Guacamole salad, 10

Ham-broccoli salad, zesty, 54
Herb(ed)
    basil-tomato vinaigrette, 65
    garlic dressing, 63
    -garlic salad, 9
    minty apple-cucumber salad, 56
    tarragon dressing, 69
Hominy salad, 33
Honey-curry dressing, 72
Horseradish–sour cream dressing, tangy, 64

Leek-mushroom salad, 21
Lemon-mustard dressing, 70
Lentil and brown rice salad, 24
Lettuce
    Bibb-mandarin salad, 20
    Caesar salad, 3–4
    romaine salad, 8
    escarole salad, 23
Lime chicken salad, 48

Mandarin-Bibb salad, 20
Marinated
    black-eyed pea salad, 25
    crab salad, 44
    green bean salad, 11
    pepper slaw, 22
    steak salad, flank, 50–51
    vegetable salad, 14
Mexican
    bean salad, 34
    dinner salad, 6
    salad bowl, 36
Minty apple-cucumber salad, 56
Moroccan carrot salad, 7
Mozzarella-tomato salad, 16
Mushroom-leek salad, 21
Mustard
    -lemon dressing, 70
    potato salad, 17

Nutmeg-orange dressing, creamy, 66

Onion
    creamy dressing, 75
    spring onion salad dressing, 69
Orange
    -nutmeg dressing, creamy, 66
    poppy seed salad dressing, 74
Oriental beef salad, 52–53

Pasta salad
    fusilli fruit, 58
    -garbanzo, 26
    layered, 28
    -salmon, colorful, 39
Pea salad
    black-eyed pea, 25
    meatless main dish, 37
Pepper dressing, creamy, 70
Pepper salad
    marinated slaw, 22
    sweet, 4
Pimiento dressing, 13
Pineapple dressing, creamy, 71
Poppy seed dressing, 66
    -orange, 74
Pork salad
    fruited, 55
    ham-broccoli, zesty, 54
Potato salad
    herb-garlic, 9
    mustard, 17
Poultry. See Chicken salad; Turkey salad

Raspberry vinegar, 67